CARIB

Published by Gallery Books
A Division of W H Smith Publishers Inc.
112 Madison Avenue
New York, New York 10016

Produced by
Brompton Books Corp.
15 Sherwood Place
Greenwich, CT 06830

ISBN 0-8317-1188-4

Printed in Hong Kong

10 9 8 7 6 5 4 3 2 1

BEAN

TEXT	JEAN CHIARAMONTE MARTIN
DESIGN	ADRIAN HODGKINS

GALLERY BOOKS
An imprint of W.H. Smith Publishers Inc.
112 Madison Avenue
New York, New York 10016

3/6 A classic Caribbean scene on Martinique:
white sand, green palm tree, blue sky, blue water.

INTRODUCTION

Think of the Caribbean, and it's hard not to smile. In this bright blue paradise, the mind goes on vacation and the senses come alive. Relax and let your senses remember the luminous blue-green sea, the crescent of pure white sand, the green palm trees swaying lazily against a deep blue sky; the shimmering rhythms of steel drums, the throb of the reggae beat, the hush of the sea at sunrise; the heat of the tropical sun, the tingle of cool sea water, the soft sand yielding to your bare feet; the delicate tinge of salt in the warm air, the heady fragrance of frangipani, the gentle spices of Creole cooking.

The ideal location for a respite from a hectic twentieth-century existence, the Caribbean offers visitors a unique opportunity—to do absolutely nothing. Take in the fresh sea air all day and watch the sun travel across the sky. If you're feeling particularly energetic, you might don flippers and a snorkel and drift quietly above the colorful world of the coral reefs. Or you might transfer yourself from your beach blanket to a large hammock suspended between tall palm trees and sip a cold, fruity rum concoction while the setting sun turns sky and water into a pastel palette. At night, back at your spot on the beach, you can watch a million stars come out, and look for shooting stars. With all this, who needs something to do?

Of course, for those who sunburn too easily to spend a whole day on the beach, the islands of the Caribbean offer a full range of tourist activities, from golf and tennis, to shopping, to sightseeing at historic sites. The volcanic islands, such as Martinique, Guadeloupe and St. Lucia, boast lush mountain ranges with rainforests, waterfalls and a colorful variety of flowers and birdlife which make for a pleasant day trip away from the beach. And if stargazing isn't your idea of nightlife, several islands, such as Puerto Rico, St. Martin and Aruba, have casinos where you can while away the hours, night and day.

The Caribbean islands became a mecca for sun-seekers only in the 1950s. Since then, many of the islands have sprouted big resorts, shopping districts, and other tourist amenities. Such developed islands as St. Thomas and St. Martin are also popular stops for the many cruise ships which ply the crystal waters of the Caribbean Sea. Some islands, such as Anguilla, Barbuda, and Tobago, remain relatively undeveloped for tourism. There are islands which cater primarily to scuba divers and snorkelers (Bonaire and the Caymans), islands which are yachting centers (Antigua and the British Virgin Islands), islands which are chic and cosmopolitan (St. Barts and Barbados), and islands which are more for the rough-and-ready traveller (St. John in the U.S. Virgin Islands, and Dominica). Each of the emerald islands in the 2000-mile-long Caribbean chain has its own special attractions, and this diversity, along with a near-perfect climate, proximity to North America, and great natural beauty, make this area one of the premier vacation destinations in the world.

When Christoper Columbus first sailed into the Caribbean nearly 500 years ago, he thought he had arrived in Asia and thus dubbed the region the West Indies. Later explorers referred to the arc of islands which separate the warm Caribbean Sea from the Atlantic Ocean as the Greater and Lesser Antilles. The Greater Antilles, at the north of the island chain, is composed of Cuba, the Caymans, Jamaica, Hispaniola (Haiti and the Dominican Republic) and Puerto Rico. To the south and east lie the Lesser Antilles, which consists of the Leeward Islands (the U.S. and British Virgin Islands, Anguilla, St. Martin/St. Maarten, St. Barts, Saba, Statia, St. Kitts, Nevis, Antigua, Barbuda, Montserrat and Guadeloupe); the Windward Islands (Dominica, Martinique, St. Lucia, Barbados, St. Vincent and the Grenadines, and Grenada); Trinidad and Tobago (off the northeast coast of Venezuela); and the Dutch ABC islands (Aruba, Bonaire, and Curacao, far west of Grenada). Bermuda, the Bahamas, and the Turks and Caicos Islands lie entirely in the Atlantic Ocean, and thus are not considered part of the Caribbean island group.

The islands of the Caribbean were originally inhabited by peaceful Arawak and warlike Carib Indians. By the sixteenth century the native population had been decimated by slavery, war and disease as European explorers, traders and pirates fought over and exploited the islands. Today, all that remains of the native population is a small group of Caribs on Dominica. By the seventeenth century Spain, England, France, Denmark and Holland had each lay claim to various islands and, using slaves imported from Africa, colonists planted the rich land with sugar cane and began reaping great fortunes. Vestiges of this age can be seen throughout the Caribbean in the form of colonial government buildings, plantation houses and the ruins of stone sugar mills.

With the abolition of slavery in the nineteenth century came the end of the age of plantations. Those who remained in the islands turned to small-scale agriculture, fishing and mining for their livelihoods. More recently, tourism has become a major industry, although not all have benefitted from it. In the past century many of the colonies have achieved political independence, causing periods of internal strife on some islands, like Jamaica. Yet the islands today retain the flavor of their colonial heritage: Spanish in the Dominican Republic and Puerto Rico; French in Guadeloupe, Martinique, St. Barts and St. Martin; British in Antigua, Barbados, the British Virgin Islands, St. Kitts and Nevis; and Dutch in Aruba, Bonaire, Curacao and St. Maarten. These European accents, combined with African influences in cuisine, music, art and ways of life, have created a distinct culture in the West Indies which varies, as does the dialect, from island to island.

Nature can sometimes be harsh, as when Hurricane Hugo hit the northern islands in September 1989 and caused extensive damage, but it is usually benevolent. Gentle tradewinds temper the heat of the tropical sun; brief showers cool the late afternoons, often leaving a perfect rainbow in a blue sky. Colorful flowers grow in profusion, and bright hummingbirds hover at the fragrant blossoms. Extensive coral reefs protect the islands during storms, and create intricate homes for an astounding variety of colorful fish. There is a slow rhythm to life on the islands, a leisurely pace which seems infinitely sensible. You easily switch into Caribbean time as soon as you arrive, but it is not so easy to switch back into fast-forward when it's time to leave. You return home with the sun in your bones, a shuffle in your walk, and a lasting smile on your face. The Caribbean has worked its magic.

BEACHES

One of the world's great destinations for beach lovers, the Caribbean boasts classic sands that look even brighter and more beautiful in real life than they do in those tempting airline posters which spring up like mushrooms every winter in the Great White North. Palm-fringed crescents of white powdery sand lapped gently by sparkling blue-green water grace most of the Caribbean islands. Among the loveliest which have been thoroughly discovered but do not host hotels are Pigeon Point on Tobago, Trunk Bay on St. John, and Magen's Bay on St. Thomas. For beachgoers who like to have hotel amenities close at hand, Negril on Jamaica, Palm Beach on Aruba, and Seven Mile Beach on Grand Cayman Island are especially spectacular strands which are partially lined by resorts. At the other end of the spectrum are the completely deserted sands of the tiny, uninhabited cays of the Grenadines and the British Virgin Islands, accessible only by yacht.

Intrepid travellers intent on finding a stretch of sand to call their own for a day can often reach paradise via a four-wheel-drive vehicle. Antigua, for example, has 365 beaches, many of which are inaccessible to the normal waves of tourist traffic. Such islands as Anguilla and Barbuda remain far enough off the beaten track to offer a full selection of stunning, unpopulated beaches to true beach bums, for whom shell-collecting and watching the ebb and flow of the tide are sufficient activity to fill a perfect day.

People-watchers often head for the French islands, where swimwear is brief and the beach scene is particularly lively. Martinique and Guadeloupe both have a Club Med as well, and St. Martin is especially popular with honeymooners and young vacationers. Members of the smart set have traditionally taken in the sun on St. Barts, Barbados, and such private resort islands as Petit St. Vincent and Palm Island in the Grenadines. Mustique is the private island haunt of such celebrities as Princess Margaret and Mick Jagger.

Of course, not all beaches are equal, even in the Caribbean. White coral sand is the most popular, along with pink coral on such islands as Barbados. Black sand beaches, the legacy of millions of years of volcanic activity, can be found on Dominica, Montserrat, St. Lucia and St. Vincent, among others. At The Baths on Virgin Gorda, in the British Virgin Islands, huge volcanic boulders on the beach form natural pools and grottoes ideal for secluded sunbathing. On Aruba, divi divi trees permanently bent by the tradewinds take the place of palm trees, and cacti decorate the dry, arid land. And although beaches on the Atlantic side of the islands tend to be a bit rougher than those on the Caribbean side, they are often no less lovely. Crane Beach on Barbados, Luquillo on Puerto Rico, and Puerto Plata in the Dominican Republic are fabulous stretches which compare favorably with the famous beaches of the Caribbean Sea.

15 Magen's Bay on St. Thomas is often rated as one of the world's most beautiful beaches.

18/19 *Green Cay in the British Virgin Islands is a lovely deserted island on which to be stranded for a day.*

21 *A sunworshipper basks on a secluded rock at The Baths.*

16/17 *Local fishing boats take daytrippers to the idyllic Ilet Pinel, off the coast of French Cul de Sac on St. Martin.*

20 *Huge boulders on the beach create private sunning places at The Baths on Virgin Gorda, British Virgin Islands.*

22/23 *Friendship Bay on the south side of the island of Bequia in the Grenadines is a haven of peace and tranquillity.*

24/25 Coconut palms line the beach at Las Terrenas, Samaná, on the Atlantic side of the Dominican Republic.

26 A dinghy floats in the turquoise waters off Marina Cay, BVI.

27 A yacht approaches Ilet Pinel, St. Martin.

28 Beautiful St. James Beach stretches along the west coast of Barbados.

29 Seven Mile Beach on Grand Cayman Island is one of the longest and most attractive beaches in the Caribbean.

30 This charming house on Cane Garden Bay
in Tortola, BVI, has its own private beach.

31 A couple enjoys one of the many secluded
beaches in the British Virgin Islands.

32 A bather emerges from the clear waters of Curacao, in the Netherlands Antilles.

33 Ahhh, paradise! A couple sunbathes on St. Thomas, in the U.S. Virgin Islands.

34 Racing along on a catamaran is a more active way to enjoy the Caribbean sun and sea.

35 Snorkelers meet a host of colorful fish in
the reefs off an uninhabited cay.

36/37 A solitary rider and a dog trot along the
shore at sunset in Montserrat.

38 A bathing beauty smiles for the camera.

39 A young lovely sits pretty on the deck of a yacht.

40/41 Admiralty Bay in Bequia is a popular mooring for peripatetic sailors cruising the Grenadines.

42 A windsurfer takes sail beneath a magnificent sunset in Anguilla.

43 A golden sun sinks behind low clouds at Boqueron, on the Caribbean coast of Puerto Rico.

44/45 Another glorious day in the Caribbean comes to a close as sunset streaks the sky with color at Palm Beach in Aruba.

NATURE

Caressed by gentle tradewinds and warmed by the tropical sun, the islands of the Caribbean are the perfect setting for some of nature's finest work. In this land of eternal summer, the rich greens of lush tropical foliage provide a constant backdrop for fabulous flowers, in every color of the rainbow, which bedeck various species all year round. Here orchids grow wild, and hibiscus needs no encouragement to bloom profusely. Tulip trees from Africa and royal poinciana flower in fiery red; bougainvillea comes out in white, purple, orange and red; and the sweet-smelling frangipani tree adds its delicate blossoms to the general riot of color in yellow, pink and red. Emerald green, turquoise blue, and ruby red hummingbirds dart among the foliage, stopping to feed now and again on the tender blossoms.

Beneath the crystal surface of the sea lies a world of coral gardens and their brightly-colored inhabitants, gently set into motion by the warm waters. Some of the best snorkeling and scuba diving in the world can be found in the Caribbean, where coral reefs and submerged wrecks provide an ideal environment for an amazing number and variety of tropical fish. Sea fans in purple, blue and pale green sway as angelfish, cardinalfish and damselfish feed on the skeletal formations of coral. Multicolored parrotfish curiously blink their turquoise eyelids at passing snorkelers. The occasional sharp-toothed barracuda, winged manta ray and slow-moving sea turtle are reminders that the reefs are much more than vast aquariums. Buccoo Reef on Tobago, Buck Island on St. Croix and the underwater trail at Trunk Bay on St. John in the U.S. Virgin Islands are known for especially good snorkeling, while the Caymans, Saba and Bonaire are favored by divers.

The growth of tourism has led many islands to create preserves and parks to protect areas of dramatic natural beauty. Two-thirds of the island of St. John is owned by the U.S. National Park Service; Puerto Rico's 28,000-acre El Yunque rainforest is part of the U.S. National Forest system; and both Martinique and Guadeloupe have a Parc Naturel which features rainforests and volcanoes. St. Lucia and St. Vincent also have volcanoes which challenge the hardy hiker, with terrain ranging from dense rainforest to steep black volcanic ridges. Guided tours take visitors up, into and through the craters, past boiling sulfur pits, bubbling mud pots and steaming fumaroles, in a landscape that seems in parts more like the moon than the tropics. Adventurous travellers in search of the unspoiled Caribbean can find it on Dominica, where small villages nestle among volcanic peaks, black sand beaches, acres and acres of lush vegetation, freshwater streams and pools, and breathtaking waterfalls.

47 Scuba divers get a fish-eye view of the underwater world at one of the coral reefs off St. John, U.S. Virgin Islands. The underwater trail at Trunk Bay is a favorite with snorkelers.

*48 A colorful queen angelfish feeds on a
bright orange brain coral at the Marine Park in
Bonaire. The coral reef which rings the entire
island of Bonaire is preserved as an
underwater park, making this one of the finest
snorkeling and scuba diving areas in the
world.*

49 A massive manta ray plies the waters of Buccoo Bay in Tobago.

50/51 Virgin Islands National Park covers two-thirds of the island of St. John. In the foreground of this aerial view is the elegant Caneel Bay, one of only two major resorts on the island.

52 top The yellow hibiscus is a cousin of the red hibiscus, which grows in profusion throughout much of the Caribbean.

52 bottom A white butterfly rests on a wild poinsettia in St. John.

53 One of the loveliest flowering plants in the Caribbean is the fragrant bougainvillea.

54/55 A spectacular rooftop view on the island of Tortola, much of which retains its natural beauty thanks to strictly limited development.

56 Children play in the waterfall at Blue Basin in Haiti.

57 Lizards are a common sight everywhere in the Caribbean.

58 Trafalgar Falls in Dominica takes a breathtaking 100-foot plunge.

59 Dozens of snowy egrets roost in a tree at twilight on Montserrat.

60/61 Much of the island of Dominica is
covered by tropical rainforest.

62 The Flower Forest in St. Joseph Parish on
Barbados is a 50-acre preserve for flowering
trees, shrubs and ferns as well as plantation
crops on which the island economy once
depended.

63 Dominica's black sand beaches are the result of volcanic activity.

64/65 A rainbow cascades over Reef Bay, St. John.

66/67 La Soufrière, on the north side of St. Vincent, last erupted in 1979.

68/69 An aerial view of the crater atop La Soufrière, St. Vincent.

70 Hikers ascend a ridge of hardened black lava as they approach the summit of St. Vincent's volcano. Note the lush foliage covering the adjacent mountainside.

71 *Plant life creeps through the pitted surface of a lava field on Anguilla.*

72 On the flat, coral islands such as Bonaire,
cacti grow as tall as 20 feet.

73 Thanks to man's intervention, cacti and
palm trees share the landscape on arid Aruba.

74 *A daytrip to Dunn's River Falls is a must for visitors to Ocho Rios, Jamaica.*

75 The sea crashes against the rugged
northern coast of Aruba.

76/77 Caribbean sunsets are magical
moments, and this one at Montego Bay,
Jamaica, is no exception.

BEYOND THE BEACHES

Although heralded primarily for fine beaches, the Caribbean has a great deal to offer those who enjoy a more active holiday. For sports enthusiasts, tennis, golf, sportfishing and yachting are excellent, while for tourists, shopping and exploring historic sites provide a pleasant day away from the sand and the sea.

Most major resorts have tennis courts suitable for casual play, but for those who want to take a more professional approach the Half Moon Club and Montego Bay Racquet Club in Jamaica, Sandy Lane in Barbados, and Palmas del Mar, the Hyatt Cerromar Beach, and Hyatt Dorado Beach in Puerto Rico have outstanding facilities. For challenging golf on spectacular courses, Casa del Campo in the Dominican Republic, Tryall in Jamaica and Mahogany Run in St. Thomas are some of the best in the Caribbean.

The northern reaches of the Caribbean have some of the finest waters for sportfishing in the world. Game fish include marlin, tuna, wahoo, pompano, and tarpon, and world-class catches have been made on charters off the Dominican Republic and Puerto Rico. Steady breezes, fair weather and accessibility to innumerable uninhabited cays and secluded coves make yachting and daysailing in the Caribbean a delight. Historic Nelson's Dockyard in Antigua is one of the most picturesque anchorages in the West Indies.

Shopping for local handicrafts and imported bargains is especially attractive in the islands, and best buys vary from island to island. Prices are often fixed in the shops and boutiques, but at marketplaces a shrewd shopper can indulge in a bit of friendly haggling with local vendors and come away with some real bargains. In general, the most coveted import bargains include crystal and china, perfume, Swiss watches, designer fashions and jewelry, while local products feature straw goods, seashells, batiks, wood carvings and rum.

Historic sites date from the colonial period and include forts, plantation houses, sugar mills and government buildings. Spanish architectural styles characterize the churches and cathedrals of Puerto Rico and the Dominican Republic. The impressive government buildings of St. Thomas and St. Croix were built by the Danes in the eighteenth and nineteenth centuries, and are now maintained by the United States. On St. Kitts, the grand fortress of Brimstone Hill, situated atop a 750-foot cliff, took the British more than a century to build. Barbados and Jamaica have some of the Caribbean's best-preserved greathouses from the plantation era, and La Pagerie, a sugar plantation on Martinique, was the birthplace of Empress Josephine, Napoleon's wife, and is now a well-maintained museum. On St. John, the ruins of the Annaberg Plantation also provide a stunning view of the British Virgin Islands across the glistening blue-green Caribbean Sea.

79 *The spectacularly-situated golf course at Mahogany Run on St. Thomas includes a green on a rocky promontory known as "The Devil's Triangle."*

*80 A haunt of the rich and famous, St. Barts'
one town, Gustavia, surrounds a picture-
perfect yacht basin.*

*81 Charter sailboats await clientele at a dock
on St. Martin.*

82/83 St. Thomas has the busiest cruise-ship harbor in the West Indies. Passengers can take advantage of the excellent duty-free shopping in Charlotte Amalie.

84/85 Nelson's Dockyard in Antigua, the headquarters of the British fleet in the eighteenth century, has been faithfully restored and remains one of the safest harbors in the world.

86 Rafts on the Rio Grande near Port Antonio, Jamaica, originally carried bananas from the plantations to freighters. Today they are a major tourist attraction.

87 Tennis is a popular activity in the cooler early-morning and late-afternoon hours. These courts are at the Hodges Bay Club in Antigua.

88 Royal palms and bougainvillea grace the
Botanical Gardens on St. Croix.

89 Established in 1765, the Botanic Gardens
on St. Vincent are the oldest in the West Indies.

90/91 A scenic drive on St. Vincent takes
visitors past a working arrowroot plantation.

92 Field hands cut sugar cane on Tortola, BVI.

93 A footbridge leads up to a restored sugar
mill on St. Croix.

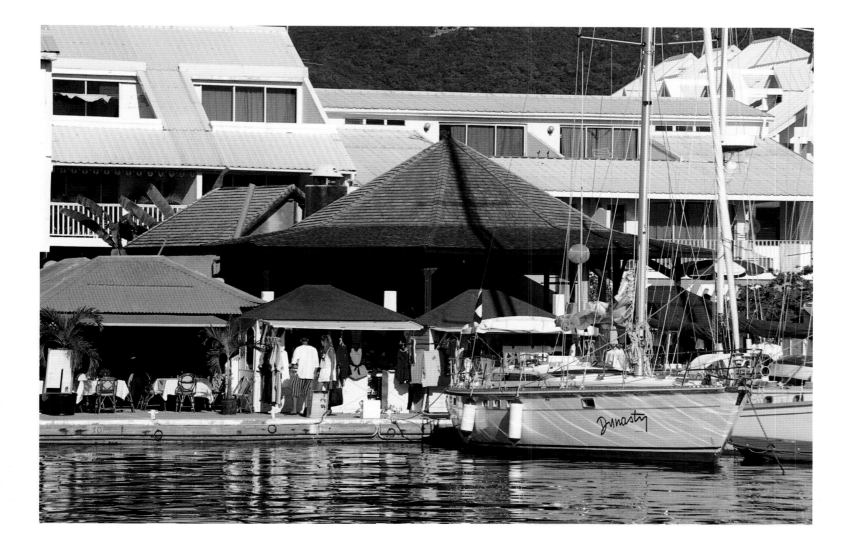

94 A boutique painted in tropical colors lures
shoppers with tempting items hung outside of
wide-open doors.

95 Shoppers browse in an open-air market at
Marigot on St. Martin.

96 *The Rose Hall Great House, three miles east of Montego Bay, Jamaica, is one of the best-kept eighteenth-century plantation houses in the islands.*

97 *An eighteenth-century cannon stands guard on the grounds of Government House in Plymouth, the capital of Montserrat.*

98/99 Willemstad, the capital of Curacao,
contains some fine examples of Dutch colonial
architecture.

100 The Spanish renaissance Cathedral de
Santa María la Menor in the Dominican
Republic, completed in 1523, is the oldest
cathedral in the western hemisphere.

101 The sixteenth-century fortress El Morro in
Old San Juan, Puerto Rico, defended San
Juan Harbor against invaders for centuries.

102 Sam Lord's Castle in Barbados, the
nineteenth-century home of the notorious
shipwrecker, is now a luxury resort.

103 Like its counterpart in London, Trafalgar Square in Bridgetown, Barbados, features a statue of Lord Nelson.

104/105 Streetlights reflect on the water at dusk in Fort-de-France, Martinique.

LOCAL COLOR

West Indian culture is as bright and colorful as the Caribbean sun and sea. Styles of music, dance, architecture, food, art and living vary from island to island, depending on the colonial and African legacy particular to each location.

Calypso, or soca, originated in Trinidad and has become the music of the islands. Sometimes accompanied by steel drums, which were originally fashioned out of oil drums, calypso combines African rhythms with improvisational tempos and rhymes. The lyrics are often humorous, and more often risqué, and the beat is happy and contagious. Reggae is the heartbeat of Jamaica. Popularized by Bob Marley, who died in 1981, reggae's heavy, pulsing bass line and often revolutionary lyrics inspire a trancelike style of dance which is nevertheless irresistible.

One of the best times to experience West Indian music and dance is during Carnival, traditionally celebrated on the two days before Lent, although some islands postpone their festivities until summer. Trinidad is especially famous for its elaborate parades and costumes at Carnival time. There is always a jump-up, where steel bands lead crowds of dancing and singing revellers through the streets.

Feasting is also an important aspect of Carnival, making this an excellent time to sample the food and drink of the islands. Tropical fruits and vegetables such as coconut, mango, papaya, plantain, breadfruit, yams and callaloo feature largely in West Indian cuisine, as does all kinds of seafood, which is plentiful in the Caribbean Sea. Styles of cooking vary from island to island, with Spanish, French, English or Dutch touches the most common, while curry, which came from India, can be found in the Creole stews and *roti* (meat pastries) prepared throughout the region. Rum, too, is ubiquitous in the islands, and each island has its own special blend of which it is proud. Distilled from sugar cane, it is especially delicious and refreshing when mixed with tropical fruit juices and drunk from a tall, frosty glass.

Some of the most memorable images of the islands come from scenes of village life. Women balance handwoven baskets of fruit on their heads on their way to the local market; a fisherman mends a net on a deserted beach at sunset; people dressed cheerily in their Sunday finest pour forth from a small white church framed by swaying coconut palms. Everything manmade—clothing, homes, market stalls, fishing boats—is brightly colored in accord with the deep blue of the sky, the rich aqua of the sea, and the rainbow hues of the brilliant blossoms which seem to grow everywhere.

107 A child's happy face is decorated with glitter for Carnival.

108 Local children pause while mending
fishing nets, Montserrat.

109 This brightly-painted fishing boat is anchored in the vivid blue waters of Barbados.

110/111 Port-of-Spain, Trinidad, is one of the
busiest working harbors in the Caribbean.

112 Lobster is one of many gastronomic treats
that comes from the rich Caribbean Sea.

113 Fresh tropical fruit is plentiful and delightful to eat in the hot Caribbean climate.

114 Farmers on St. Thomas bring their fruits
and vegetables to the local dock for
transportation to Charlotte Amalie.

115 In Haiti, women still carry their goods to
market in large handwoven baskets which they
balance on their heads.

116 A house on Tortola is gaily painted in purple and yellow.

117 A bright green door in Tortola.

118/119 The whitewashed walls of a nursery school on St. Thomas are spruced up with hand-painted palm trees, houses, birds and fish.

120/121 Brightly-dressed churchgoers
disperse after Sunday mass on a sunny
January morning.

122 Locals play dominoes with great energy,
often slamming the dominoes down on the
table for extra emphasis. Groups of spectators
usually gather to watch the action.

123 Cricket is played on all of the British islands. This game is taking place in Buff Bay, Jamaica.

124/125 The Jamaican Constabulary Marching Band parades in Port Royal.

126 A young boy in costume waits for his turn
to join in the Carnival parade.

127 Hundreds of paraders in elaborate,
glittery costumes fill the streets at the highlight
of Carnival.